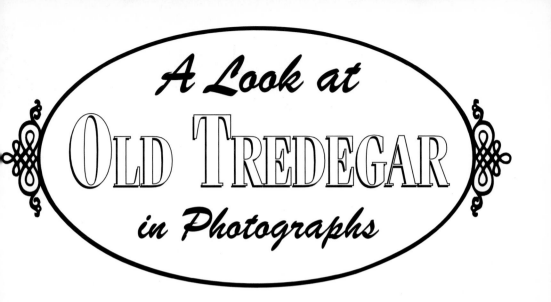

A Look at OLD TREDEGAR in Photographs

Philip Prosser

**Foreword by
Dr. K.M. Wheeler**

Volume 2

Old Bakehouse Publications

Abertillery

© Philip Prosser

First published in October 1998
Reprinted in February 1999

ISBN 1 874538 81 6

Published in the U.K. by
Old Bakehouse Publications
Church Street,
Abertillery, Gwent NP3 lEA
Telephone: 01495 212600 Fax: 01495 216222

Made and printed in the UK
by J.R. Davies (Printers) Ltd.

Foreword
by
Dr. K.M. Wheeler

After the enormous success of Volume One of A Look at Old Tredegar in Photographs, it is a pleasure and a privilege to be asked to write a foreword to the long-awaited Volume Two. Again, this is the result of further diligent and detailed research by the author.

The original format, of depicting scenes and events from every part of the town has been maintained, and once more provides stimulating debate. It is fitting in this year of 1998 that, our town's unique heritage - Bedwellty Park, House, and Town Clock are again featured; they have been the venues for the main celebrations of the 50th Anniversary of Aneurin Bevan, Tredegar's greatest son, reminding us that as Minister of Health and Housing in the post-war Labour Government, it was he who introduced the N.H.S. on 5th July 1948.

Looking at the photographs brings happy memories of our family life, particularly of my work as a family doctor and the many friends made during fifty years in Tredegar. The author, Phil Prosser is to be warmly congratulated on this further compilation of photographs. All aspects of life are illustrated over a period of many years, and much nostalgic pleasure is provided for all those who regard Tredegar as their home town.

I commend this book and wish every success that it well deserves.

Dr. K.M. Wheeler

Contents

Introduction

Some eight years have passed since Volume One of this series of books concerning Tredegar was first published and much has happened during that relatively short space of time.

A few more historic landmarks have disappeared forever, to be replaced by new landscapes and modern environs; these events well justify the publication of books such as this and provide timely reminders of constant changes to our surroundings. Tredegar town centre has received some long overdue improvements, particularly in the pedestrianisation of Commercial Street. On a sadder note however, a once-prized landmark, the Workmen's Hall was demolished in 1995 after more than 130 years, only to be replaced by an uninviting car park.

The largest construction project in recent times has been the creation of the by-pass road from Heathfield to Nantybwch. Seen as essential to alleviate traffic congestion, the excavation work managed to reveal a number of interesting relics from Tredegar's historic mining past and the local museum has benefited from this.

Also included are photographs of numerous people and personalites who are to be remembered. Such organisations as the prestigious Orpheus Choir and Amateur Dramatic Society get a mention and some traditional, yet memorable school and chapel pictures will also catch the eye.

The year 1998 is one of celebration, with the 50th anniversary of The National Health Service. The 'Father' of this institution, the exalted Aneurin Bevan was born and bred in Tredegar, a fact that has brought much pride to our town and there are pictures of 'Nye' included in this volume.

The book contains a collection of photographs covering a variety of topics, each one intent on reviving memories of a pleasant past. The final chapter however is purposely confined to a small selection of photographs from the past and present. It is this chapter above all, which will remind us once again of the continuous pattern of change that takes place all around us, quite often without even being realised.

Finally I should like to thank everyone who willingly gave their time and assistance in producing this second volume, which I trust will be as well received and enjoyed as the first.

Philip Prosser.

P. H. Prosser

3. Castle Street in 1904 and the traffic is confined to a lone horse and cart parked outside the old Temperance Hotel. On the opposite side of the street are not so temperate places of refreshment and hostelry, the Cambrian Hotel and the King's Head Inn.

4. Looking up Morgan Street towards the clock during the depressive years of the early 1930s. The pace of life appears to be very quiet in Tredegar during this period with menfolk standing around and little traffic to concern them.

5. A tree-lined North Avenue in Ashvale pictured here in the late 1930s soon after the houses had been constructed and occupied for the first time. Today's residents will notice a few changes particularly some modernised street-lighting since this picture was taken.

6. Another view from the 1930s and this time looking up a very peaceful Church Street. On the right, behind an antiquated lamppost is the former garage of Percy Evans. On the opposite side of the road and just in view is the porch of the North Western Hotel which was also known as The Miners.

7. An almost deserted Market Street with two prominent old-fashioned business signs. On the left is a protruding striped pole revealing that this shop was a barbers or hairdressers as known in this age. On the opposite corner of the street the building displays a sign holding three small orbs, the indication that this was a pawnbroker's shop, a trade which has all but disappeared these days. The building today is the site of the Old County Club.

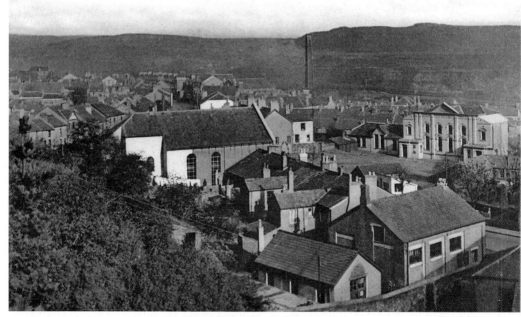

8. A general view of the town taken from Park View which shows the old fire station in the foreground. In the background is one of the chimney stacks belonging to the Tredegar Iron and Coal Company's works.

9./10. These are two views of an ever changing Commercial Street in Tredegar. Above, the year is 1904 and shows the once substantial boot and shoe shop of Briggs on the corner. Shoes are on offer in the sale at 6/11 (35p). Below, the years have moved on to the 1930s and just a little further up the street on the right, a selection of cycle tyres is displayed outside S.L. Thomas the ironmongers.

11. A look down Castle Street during the early 1900s. These were the days when the Castle Hotel boasted a most ornate balustrade.

12. A scene not easily recognisable these days is the view of the yard gates at the top of Church Street. The period is the late 1940s and an old Red and White bus makes its way into town.

13. When this picture was taken, the old cottages in Charles Street had already been abandoned by their owners to make way for re-development. The doors and windows are all bricked up but the nearby public house, the Coach and Horses has survived. The site seen here is now occupied by a nursing home.

14. Probably photographed during the 1950s, the view is looking up Georgetown Hill. The large building at the bottom right will be remembered as the old Police Station.

15. Another old Tredegar street that has since disappeared is High Street as pictured here shortly before its demise. Seen on the left of the photograph and already in a demolished state, are the remains of Rees's corner shop.

16. The photographs in this book cover a wide span of the twentieth century and make interesting comparisons during different periods. This view of Church Street is from about 1902 and just visible in the background are the arches of the old Sirhowy Ironworks.

17. By today's standards, Albert Terrace would fall well short of what is required and expected. However, built in the 1840s as accommodation for workers of the Sirhowy colliers and iron-workers, the cottages were to serve many happy families for well over a hundred years. Things of the past, such as outside toilets, whitewashed walls and open baileys or yards are typical of 19th century workers' housing in South Wales.

18. Blaencwm Viaduct or the Nine Arches as it became known with Nantybwch Station in the distance.

19./20. Two photographs from ninety years ago illustrating a number of Tredegar farms. The scene above is of Garn Ddu Farm situated near Nantybwch Waterworks. Below can be seen Blaencwm Farm Nantybwch with its partly-thatched roof. Also to be seen in the centre is Tai Bach with Tynewydd at the top left and Penrhyn on the right.

21. Nantybwch, which has changed somewhat since this picture of 1960 with much redevelopment having taken place. The Crown Inn and Cosh's Garage are two of the prominent buildings.

22. Ashvale House at Nantybwch pictured when it served as the local isolation hospital. The premises now form the site of the Aneurin Bevan Home For The Elderly.

23. The once-elegant dwelling of The Grove near Sirhowy Bridge pictured many years ago whilst still in private hands. The building these days will be better recognised as the Social Services Office.

24. A dismal day's weather at the Circle in about 1955. These were the days when it was used as the town's main bus stop and on the right is seen a 'double decker' waiting to leave for Ebbw Vale.

25. The bottom end of Church Street with trees and ivy adorning the houses. On the right is Jones's Goytre Shop which in later years went on to become the premises of the Democratic Club.

26. This Tredegar book contains a number of photographs of former busy streets of the town. This is Bridge Street which was the main shopping area of Tredegar during the early 1800s. The above picture will be familiar to many readers, it being photographed shortly before demolition.

27. From the 1920s comes this photograph of Park View with the mountain road to Rhymney in the background.

28. At one time hillsides surrounding Tredegar were totally rural and scattered with farms. Above is Shon Shefrey Farm which was situated just north of Nantybwch Reservoir and now lies in ruins.

29. Here is the long barn of Glan Rhyd Uchaf or perhaps better known as Robbins Farm. In the background is Minyrafon but more familiarly known as 'The Huts'. This once farmland is now the site of the Dukes Meadow Housing Estate.

30. The bottom end of Tredegar in 1950. To be seen are Vale Terrace, the Gas Works and the Grammar School to the right. To the far right is Mount Pleasant. In the foreground are further strong reminders of the past such as the railway lines and a large stock of wooden pit props for use in nearby Tŷ Trist Colliery.

31. In this early general view can be seen the Tredegar Iron & Coal Company offices with the old stables on the left.

36. The matron, staff and colleagues at the General Hospital probably pictured during the 1940s. The hospital was built in 1903 long before the introduction of the National Health Service. Until such time the health and well-being of the population of Tredegar relied on the scheme provided by the Tredegar Workmen's Medical Aid Society. For a weekly contribution of a few pence, members and their families were provided with full medical services.

37. Castle Street pictured during the early 1930s and well-decorated to celebrate the annual 'Hospital Week'. Local hospitals would not have survived in these depressing years without the support volunteered by the public.

38. An aerial view showing a few local landmarks to be noted. To the left is the bus station, centre is the Forge Pond with part of the Tredegar Works on the right.

39. This is a view taken from an old picture postcard describing it as the top of the Sirhowy Valley showing the mountains. Prominent in the foreground is Bracty Farm, originally an ale house which was frequented by thirsty workers during the building of the Nine Arches. The older name was Ty-Morgan Howells, Bracty being the Welsh name for ale house.

40. The now disappeared bus station with the popular and sizeable eleven-table Lucania snooker hall in the background. The modern-day shopping precinct now occupies this area.

41. Probably the most photographed landmark in the town in years gone by was the prestigious clock. This picture taken at the Circle in 1908 shows its old surround with four gas standards. Some latter day businesses include Charles and Finch the ironmongers on the right, two public houses the Freemason's Arms and the Black Prince on the left, together with Tom Price's grocery stores.

42. A post Second World War shortage saw the country's demand for new and better housing far outstrip the means of supply. The answer was to be found in the erection of fast assembly and economical pre-fabricated dwellings: to be known to one and all as 'the Prefabs'. The Arkon type seen here was initially designed to have a maximum life span of ten years. However they became so popular and comfortable dwellings in many areas they were to be occupied for more than three times their life expectancy. In some parts of the country, there was emotive protest from the occupants when told by local councils they were to be re-housed in 'better homes'. The photograph above was taken in July 1946 at Nantybwch and now forms the site of the Community Hall.

43. Temple Street, which was built on a slope stemming off Church Street leading to the wall supporting the railway lines belonging to the T.I.C. (Tredegar Iron & Coal Company). Some readers may remember the popular bakery at the bottom of this street. These days, the council flats of Church Street fill the site.

44. The construction of the A465 (Heads of the Valley Road) in the early 1960s was a massive project that changed the landscape in northern Monmouthshire enormously. At the time of publication of this book there are plans afoot, some controversial, to expand the carriageway even further. In the upper photograph the retaining wall near Tafarnaubach is under construction in 1965. The houses seen here were eventually demolished.

45. Another scene at old Tafarnaubach with some motor vehicles passing over the railway bridge. The bungalows in the background have since been removed and the area is now the location of Bryn Bach Park.

46./47. These are two further scenes of the former landscape that once was, and now much more difficult to remember. Above can be seen Penmark, Dukestown and the remains of the railway line passing between the gates, now forms the route of the A465. The lower picture shows the remains of Nantybwch Station and the lifting of the track in 1964.

48. Progress is now being made in the road construction by 1966. Building of the bridge over the weir below the Nine Arches is nearing completion.

49. A picturesque scene at Bedwellty Park in about 1923 showing the 'Ladies Shelter', a segregated building it would appear, in those days. Of interest on the right of the picture is a German field gun recovered from the battlefields of the First World War (1914-1918). The symbolic display of captured enemy weapons was popular around the country at the time, until more fitting War Memorials were built.

50. Passenger travel by bus was growing in popularity by the 1920s and here is a group of Valley Buses. They are parked in Church Street which was used as their base throughout the 1920s and 1930s.

51. Passenger travel by train is a luxury which has not been available in the Tredegar district for almost forty years. Here, in the early 1950s a train heads for Nantybwch Station over the Nine Arches, Blaencwm Viaduct.

52. Tredegar as viewed from the air with many landmarks since gone such as Whitworth Pit at the bottom of the picture together with the company offices and stables.

CHAPTER 2

Churches & Chapels

53. Changing attitudes and diminishing religious allegiance have compelled very many closures and destruction of former places of worship throughout the country. Above is a surviving photograph of Bethania Chapel (1874-1974), which once stood on the road leading to Troedrhiwgwair.

54. St. David's Church at Troedrhiwgwair with the minister and members of the choir. Seen left to right are: Front row - Ralph Tuck, Hugh Thomas, Mr. Jones, Luther Evans, Mr. Morgan and Charles Turner. Middle row - Hugh Jones, Oswald Thomas, Dick Sadler, Ken Thomas, Cyril Lewis, Anthony Rees and Stan Turner. Back row - Les Thomas, Melvin Thomas and Ray Thomas.

55. The Primitive Methodist Chapel which was situated in Commercial Street. This church served the worshippers for almost a century before eventual closure and demolition during the early 1960s. The site was cleared to make way for the bus station.

56. Always a popular annual event was the 'chapel outing' to the seaside. These are members of Picton Street United Reformed Chapel and a few names are known. Back row - Ken Isles, John McQuade, unknown and Gwyn Williams. Middle row - Maureen Jones, Wanda James, unknown, unknown and Jean Morgan. Third row - Carrie Beeks, Stella Beeks, Agnes Parry and Iris Parry. Unfortunately the author has been unable to trace the two ladies in the front row. The church was pulled down in 1993 to be replaced by a supermarket.

57. Saron Congregational which was first built in the year 1819, to be rebuilt in 1828 and again in 1858 still survives to this day. The street was at one time known as Chapel Street; this was due to the fact that there were four places of worship all in close proximity.

58. Members of the now demolished Tabernacle Sunday School Dukestown stop for the photographer during a Whitsun Walk in about 1908. The houses on the left are St. Clear's Place and on the far right can be seen St. George's Parish Hall. Unfortunately only the vestry remains of the Tabernacle, which is still used by the faithful few.

59. This is a Whitsun Parade by the members of Poplar Road Congregational Sunday School during the 1950s. Many readers should be able to name a few familiar faces seen here. The chapel still remains in use as the Gospel Hall.

60. The Salvation Army was founded in 1865 by William Booth. The movement is now a worldwide Christian organisation and has a steady following in Tredegar. Above, is a photograph of the Tredegar band, comprising of twenty-five members during the period of around 1910.

61. Another one-time favourite chapel of many was Elim Congregational which stood at the top of Salisbury Street. Elim was opened in 1854 but unfortunately it is pictured in a 'sorry state' here in 1986, in the process of being demolished. The site is now occupied by housing known as Town Houses.

62. The pupils of Carmel Sunday School during an anniversary walk in 1967.

Carmel Baptist Chapel Dukestown - The Early Years

Carmel has a history that can be traced back almost three centuries. It was during the reign of Charles I that nonconformist religion gained momentum throughout Wales; a situation barely tolerated by the English Parliament. Secret worship would take place in private homes amid fears of brutal persecution. By 1800, with the development of the coal workings and iron industry at Sirhowy and Tredegar, the population multiplied rapidly. The Baptist movement was to prove to be the most popular of nonconformist religions; history records in particular, the Baptists of Sirhowy as being brave pioneers of dissent in Wales.

In 1833 it became necessary for the faithful to have a place of their own in which to worship. Not without problems, land on which to build was eventually acquired from the Duke of Beaufort's estate.

This was met with a period of fierce opposition from a certain James Williams and his wife, keepers of a nearby public house The Moulders Arms. The lady in question was said to possess an 'inexhaustible supply of bad temper'. Her objections to the use of nearby land for the building of a chapel centered on the problem of where else could she now send her drunken customers to lie down and sleep! However, influential agents for the Duke of Beaufort intervened and the building of Carmel commenced in the summer of 1834.

The grand opening took place on May 12th 1835 with ministers from all corners of Monmouthshire gathering to preach the word. The first full-time appointed minister was Rev. David Roberts of Rhymney. As years went by, so the congregations began to swell and major extensions took place in 1853, with the chapel being lengthened by fifteen feet.

Like many institutions over the years old tradition died hard and a number of such issues are recorded at Carmel. Until 1903 Welsh was the only spoken tongue in all of the chapel's services. Then much to the consternation of the elders and puritans, English was introduced to certain parts of the Sunday evening service; it was 1919 before Welsh was finally abandoned altogether. Another event, again not to find favour with many, was the purchase of the first organ in 1884; why they asked, should a 50 year-old harmonium be discarded for a modern organ contraption costing a princely £28? In the earliest days of chapel worship, 'class distinction' was an accepted fact. It was customary to charge members a quarterly rent for the use of a chapel pew; the amount of rent depending on the position of the pew and its closeness to the pulpit. The favourite hymn Nearer My God To Thee was probably sung with much determination in Carmel in early days.

The chapel had been built for some 85 years before marriages were allowed to be solemnized; the first wedding taking place in March 1920 between Mr and Mrs George Jones. As so often is the case, great numbers of devotional establishments have closed their doors forever but against all the odds Carmel Chapel has survived and still has a devout following.

63. Probably the earliest known photograph of the original Penuel Presbyterian Church after the building was converted into some cottages in 1828.

64. Penuel Welsh Calvinistic Methodist Chapel which used to stand in Harcourt Terrace. Penuel was one of the oldest church buildings in the district, the first building being erected in the year 1809. It was re-designed and re-constructed a number of times during its long history; the photograph above illustrates its appearance in 1951. At the time of publication of this book, the site of this former chapel awaits re-development.

65. The Minister and church elders of Penuel in 1951. Left to right, back row - George White, Pryce Williams, Evan Hopkins, D.D. Williams and Trevor Morgan. Front row - Evan Morgan, R.L. Thomas, Rev. D.G. Silvanus, W.H. Martin and Mrs. W.H. Martin.

66. A church group pictured outside St. Davids Church Troedrhiwgwair with a few familiar faces. The minister at the time was Rev. Luther Evans and the ladies are Mabel Thomas, Mary Ann Sadler, Blodwen Lloyd, Nancy Ellaway and Harriet Bethal. The gentlemen include Bill Bethal, Rees Bevan, Tom Healey, Mr. Gerrard, Ivor Tuck, Hugh Thomas and Ned Bevan.

67. Pictured on a day's outing are some of the members of St. James's Church Tredegar. Many names are known. Front row - Mrs. Hayward, Mrs. Milne, Mrs. Roland Davies, Mrs. Webb, Mrs. Jones, unknown and Mrs. Wilmott. Second row - Mrs. Tom Cole, Mrs. George Davies, Mrs. Jones (The Vach), Mrs. Sarah Jones, unknown and Mrs. Baxter. Third row - Mrs. Shore, unknown, unknown, Mr. Roland Davies, Mrs. Mullen, unknown, Mrs. Long and Mrs. Bond. Back row - Rev. James, unknown, Rev. Noel Jones and Mr. Tom Cole.

68. The members of the Wesleyan Chapel Scwrfa pause for a photograph at Ashvale. The chapel was opened in 1851 but fell victim to closure in 1976.

CHAPTER 3

Industrial Heritage

69. A photograph that well illustrates the back-breaking task of digging for coal with shovel and pick. Pictured with their 'tools of the trade' are left, Mr. Harry Oliver, Jim Oliver the young lad and on the right is believed to be Mr. Walter Badham.

70. The Thomas Richards Mining and Technical Institute. This was opened in 1935 as a school for boys only and provided education in the fields of metalwork, woodwork and technical drawing etc. This was essential training for school leavers of the day to prepare themselves for industrial careers. The building is now used by the Gwent Education Authority.

71. Engine Pit Sirhowy which was the property of the Ebbw Vale Company, was situated at the entrance to Sirhowy Brickworks. Sinking to a depth of 107 yards (98 metres) Engine Pit was the first colliery in the Sirhowy Valley to make use of steam to operate its winding gear. It is only in recent times (1997) that the shaft was finally capped.

72. A busy scene at Tŷ Trist Colliery where wagons loaded with coal are waiting to be checked through the weighbridge. Tŷ Trist, originally owned by the T.I.C. was amongst the longest serving pits in the valley. With its twin shafts, coal was mined here from 1834 until eventual closure in 1959.

73. A look inside the former fitting shop at Tŷ Trist. On the left is fitter Mr. Frank Hanbury with his apprentice Jim Freeman, who are in the process of constructing a coal cutter.

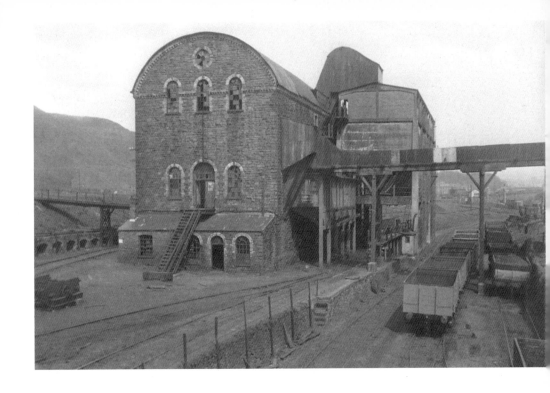

74./75. Two interesting views of the lower end of Tredegar and the former workings of Tŷ Trist. The domed building is the coal washery which was added to the colliery in 1892, and hailed as the finest plant in South Wales. The intricate machinery was revolutionary, replacing the old system whereby so much valuable quality coal was being mixed with shale and discarded.

76. Pictured in the 1970s is the entrance to the former Whitworth Drift Mine. Just visible on the right are the former company stables. At the top of the mound is the old stand on the recreation ground.

77. London and North Western Locomotive No.1949, King Arthur is seen here having been serviced at Tredegar sheds. The sheds were quite substantial here with four covered roads. The date of the picture is uncertain, but, as there are numerous female workers and youths, it may well have been during the 1914 -1918 War period when adult able men were at the Front.

49

78. The locomotive 'Graham' was one of the locos owned by Tredegar Iron & Coal Company and used around the works, shunting materials. Two of the gentlemen identified are Mr. J.H. Jones the driver and Mr. G. Daniels who is sat on the step.

79. The General Strike of 1926 brought much of the country to a standstill and hardship for thousands of families. This picture was taken at the Patches and shows some desperate locals searching for coal waste to keep their fires burning.

80. A scene at Tŷ Trist Colliery that will evoke a few memories for former workers there. The pit pony was once an essential member of the workforce at many pits both above ground and down under. Horses were used for haulage in the industry up until the 1970s before total mechanisation took over. The T.I.C. employed 650 animals during its heyday.

81. Another pit once owned by the Ebbw Vale Company was Graham's Navigation Colliery. It was originally called Edward James's First Class Pit after its founder, a local expert in pit sinking. It later adopted the more familiar title of No.9 Pit and was situated near Georgetown.

82./83. Groups of workers of the T.I.C. have time to be photographed. Above, in the year 1926 are the boilermakers and blacksmiths; below are the craftsmen and boys at the wagon repair shop. The original Tredegar Iron Company was formed in 1800 and in 1873 was restructured into the Tredegar Iron and Coal Company, developing into a huge undertaking in the Sirhowy and Rhymney Valleys. This shaped the economy of the valleys for 150 years.

84. Further down the Sirhowy Valley from Tŷ Trist was Pochin Colliery. The first coal was brought to the surface here on April 10th 1880, the last was in 1965.

85. A landmark photograph taken of Pochin Colliery from the 'Rocking Stone' in 1954.

86./87. The 'age of steam' first came to Wales in 1803 with the first locomotive being put into operation at Penydarren Works. The first such machine to be used at Tredegar arrived in 1829 and was used on the Sirhowy Tramroad. Above is a picture of a derelict 19th century Tredegar locomotive. The lower photograph was taken at the back of Brompton Place in 1928; the young lad is Mr. Alan Hayward and the lady Miss Thelma Lewis.

88. Before the realisation of electricity, coal-gas was the wonder fuel to replace oil and candles in the home. Gas was first introduced to Tredegar in 1838 by a Mr. David Morris with the building of his own mini gas works in Bridge Street. So successful was his venture, that he formed a company with a number of local traders to expand the works and light up the town. The photograph above is of Tredegar Councillors at the gasworks in 1957. Some of the names known are Tom Lucas, Charlie Hill, Don Lancastle, John Parry-Jones, Alan Baines, Rev. Ralph Jones, Billy Clark, Eddy Jones, Len Filer, Oliver Jones, Billy Bevan, Bill Watkins and Bill Lewis.

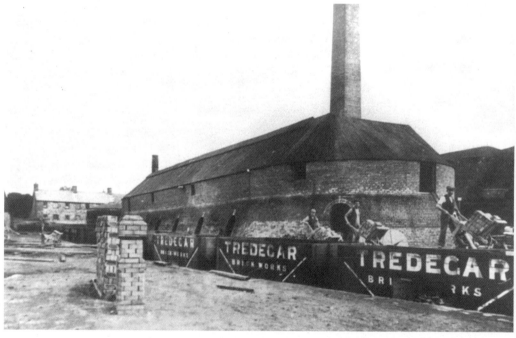

89. Busy times as bricks are being loaded from the Tredegar Brickworks. In the background can be seen Forge House.

90. To imagine where the railway lines once ran in Tredegar is very difficult these days. The passenger train above is seen approaching Sirhowy Station with the Technical School on the right; St. George's Place is on the left. To assist younger readers Sirhowy Station was situated on the ground now occupied by the ambulance station.

91. Nantybwch Station which was opened on the line from Brynmawr in 1864. Here, in the 1950s a train is arriving at the station from Abergavenny, on its way to Dowlais and Merthyr. The lines and platform on the right lead in the direction of Tredegar and on down the valley to Newport. All that remains of this scene is the row of houses on the left of the picture.

92./93. The bridge and level crossing at Tredegar Station below the busy engine sheds. The Sirhowy Railway Act of May 1860 provided legislation for the old tramway which was used to convey minerals to the Monmouthshire Canal, to be converted into a railway line. The line was eventually opened in June 1865 and provided the first passenger train service to Newport, operated by the Sirhowy Railway Co; the undertaking being taken over by the L.N.W.R. in 1876. The service came to an end in June 1960 with freight traffic lingering on until 1969.

94. Workers for Tredegar Urban District Council pose with their brand new refuse collection truck. On the left is Mr. Chris Roberts and centre is Mr. Cyril Hughes. The author apologises for being unable to identify the third member of the crew.

95. Unfortunately it has not been possible to trace the names of the three gentlemen seen on the left; they are however some members of staff pictured at Sirhowy Station, probably during the 1930s. The next stop up the line from Sirhowy was the bleak station at Nantybwch which was situated at 1165 feet (355 metres) above sea level. The line between Sirhowy and Nantybwch was opened for passenger traffic in November 1868 and enabled the population of Tredegar to travel on to Abergavenny. The line was extended in the opposite direction, linking Nantybwch to Rhymney Bridge and beyond in 1871.

96. Members of the staff of LCR Electrical Components waiting to board an aircraft for a visit to Germany in 1970. At this time this company occupied the old T.I.C. offices at the bottom of Stable Lane.

97. The T.I.C. works pictured during booming years, the greatest job provider of the town. Emanating from the first furnace at Sirhowy in 1778, the company was created by three partners Messers Fothergill, Monkhouse and Samuel Homfray of Penydarren. So important did the works become that through the nineteenth century, the town was always to be known as Tredegar Iron Works instead of plain Tredegar.

98. Possibly this picture is an opportunity for a few ladies of the former Denex Factory to be remembered during the 1950s. Situated at Ashvale the company was a clothing manufacturer. Now closed, the site is occupied by a plastics factory.

99. The skills and abilities were comprehensive at the T.I.C as witnessed in this picture from 1919. The workers in the sawmill are seen with a load of heavy timber ready for cutting into six-inch thick slabs for the sides of the company's coal trucks.

100. An aerial view of the former N.C.B. works which has since disappeared along with the collieries it once served.

101. Pictured inside the N.C.B. Foundry are Back row, left to right - Gordon Thomas, Tom Mullalieu, Dennis Jones, Clary Davies and Milton Fear. Front row - Fred Jones, Dennis Watkins and Gordon Morgan.

102. A further photograph from the N.C.B. works, this time it is the turn of the winding shop. Some of the lads are Bernard Stevens, Howard Morris, Steve Payne, Nigel Davies, Alan Francis, Chris Osland, Philip Morgan, George Starr, Bill Bennett, Keith Lewis, Gerald Davies and Howard Miles.

103. A group from the blacksmith's shop includes amongst others Clive Bufton, Basil Jones, Alan Thomas, Ray George, Albert Marsden and Wyndham Badham.

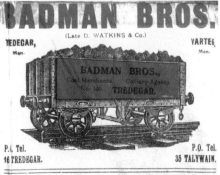

104. Above, is recorded a visit to one of the local collieries by a group of officials. The period is uncertain but the headgear and lamps have an antiquated look about them.

105. Tŷ Trist Colliery showing its three sets of winding gear. Tŷ Trist was just one of twenty collieries owned by the T.I.C. and during their peak, were producing more than a million tons of coal per annum.

CHAPTER 4

People & Events

106. At a special event at the Recreation Ground, a few members of the former Urban District Council of Tredegar are gathered at the microphone. They include Mr. Stockton, Mr. Tippings, Mr. Rawle and Mr. Wilcox.

107. Inside the council chamber at Bedwellty House. Some well known faces include Albert Scott, Ron Watkins, Angus Donaldson. Mr. Quick, Bill Thomas, reporter and Rees Davies.

108. Tredegar Carnival Queen with her eight ladies in waiting pictured during the 1940s. The throne is actually carved 'Fochriw' so it was probably borrowed for the occasion from the nearby Rhymney Valley village.

109. The occasion is the official opening of Pontywedo Bridge over the Sirhowy river below Nine Arches, Nantybwch. The date is July 30th 1930 and about to cut the tape is Alderman Thomas Davies.

110. Guests and dignitaries are poised in readiness to enjoy the annual dinner of Tredegar's Kentucky Minstrels at Bedwellty House in 1954.

111. A 'street party' scene at Rhoslan, Sirhowy which is likely to have been held to celebrate the Queen's Coronation in June 1953.

112./113. Two photographs epitomizing times of strife and struggle that once cast a shadow over life in Tredegar. The 1920s were strike-ridden years, followed by the 'hungry thirties' with incredible levels of unemployment. In the photograph above the folk are waiting for potatoes at Oakey's shop in Upper Coronation Street. Notice Ebenezer Chapel on the right where the fire station is today. In the picture below are seen the volunteers of Picton Street and their soup kitchen.

114. The St. John's Ambulance Service, a much respected institution. The group here are pictured outside Bedwellty House probably during the 1950s.

115. A troop of Brownies and Guides with some more senior members during the late 1950s.

116./117. Two photographs of special occasions attended by long serving member of Parliament for the constituency, Aneurin Bevan. Above, the occasion is the unveiling of a plaque to mark the centenary of the town clock on May 10th 1958. The ceremony is being performed by Tredegar's Mayor Mr. Bill Phillips who is accompanied by Etty Phillips, Jennie Lee (wife of Mr. Bevan), Lord Raglan, Mr. Stockton and Mr. Dai Richards.
The lower photograph was taken during the late 1940s or early 1950s and shows Mr. Bevan having just crowned the town's Carnival Queen.

118.   The districts of Tredegar and nearby Ebbw Vale have been favoured with a number of powerful politicians over the years, all with traditional Labour allegiance. In the photograph below the personalities include Michael Foot, former MP for Ebbw Vale and Blaenau Gwent and leader of the Labour Party from 1980 to 1983. On his left are, Westminster MP Llew Smith and Euro MP Glenys Kinnock.

This picture was taken at the unveiling of a plaque at No.10 Morgan Street to mark the former residence of Mr. Foot. On the opposite page can be seen Aneurin Bevan or 'Nye' as he will probably be best remembered. Nye was born and bred in Charles Street Tredegar in 1897 and left school at the age of fourteen to become an errand boy for a local butcher.

When a year or two older, he went to work at one of the local collieries; what better way was there to learn the values of comradeship and to understand the needs and aspirations of the working man? His next move was to attend the Central Labour College with dreams of a Labour influence on local politics and beyond. This was the period of the First World War, times dominated by a Liberal Government, the first Labour administration not coming to power until 1924. As the years progressed, a Labour controlled council was formed in Tredegar in 1928 with Nye Bevan being elected to Westminster as member for the Ebbw Vale constituency in 1929. Serving as the Minister of Health in the Labour Government from 1945 to 1951, it was he who was instrumental in establishing the National Health Service in this country. However the great political blow came in 1951 when, as Minister of Labour, his government proposed for the first time, the introduction of prescription charges. This was seen as an act of vandalism on Nye Bevan's dream of free medicines for all and so he resigned his post. Forever outspoken yet faithful he served his party and constituents until an untimely death at the age of 63 in 1960.

119. The Tredegar Orpheus which was originally formed in 1909, seen here at Ebbw Vale Leisure Centre. At the front are Conductor Ieuan L. Davies and accompanist Maureen Dalimore.

120. The Orpheus Choir pictured in September 1997 during a memorable visit to Switzerland. Conductor and accompanist are Ian and Helen Waite.

121. In September 1975 the Tredegar Choral Society was forced to disband due to lack of male support. The lady members however decided to take action of their own under the chairmanship of the late Mrs. L. Williams. After much hard work they eventually formed the Tredegar Choir in January 1976 under the musical directorship of Mary Watkins with Merle Johnson as accompanist. They are now better known as the Tremaryon Singers, the name created from the name of their home town and the first name of their musical director.

122. The Heads of the Valley Festival Choir which was formed in 1990. Sat in the front are the founders Tom Brown, Nigel Weeks and Enid Middleton.

123. The young 'Cub Scouts' pictured here will now be grown men, yet able to recognise themselves perhaps. The photograph was taken outside the Scout hut on Farmers Hill Dukestown in about 1950.

124. 1925 saw the end of Government subsidies on coal, following which, the coal-owners announced a reduction in wages and longer working hours. The proclamation 'not a penny off the pay or a minute on the day' came forth and set the scene for the start of a miners' strike in April 1926. By May 3rd the whole country was at a standstill for the nine-day General Strike. It was a further five months before the miners returned to work following great hardship. Pictured above is another 'soup kitchen' set up in Tredegar to help feed the hungry.

125. Tŷ Trist Colliery in about 1957 when a visiting tenor from the island of Malta toured the colliery. Seen here are, left to right: Dick Thomas, Sam Oliver, Jock Douglas, Alan Williams, Tom McCarthy, Dino Faretinos (Tenor), Ken Gale, Tom Hutchings and Arthur Williams (Pit Manager).

126./127. Two group photographs of the Merrymakers. This was a troupe formed by local boys and girls who were popular entertainers, particularly favoured at Tredegar's Workmen's Hall during its heyday of presenting stage shows.

128. No town should be without its own 'Town Band'. This is the Tredegar ensemble pictured with some trophies, and at a time when there appears to be just one female musician, at the back during the 1950s. The band is still as popular today, having accumulated many awards over the years.

129. This is a picture from the beginnings of the successful 'Little Theatre' in 1962. The cast on stage have just performed in the play *'They Came to a City'*.

131. Most of the town's cultural activities emanated from the prestigious Workmen's Hall, an institution that was the great provider of local entertainment in years gone by. The Dramatic Society was formed in 1946 and went on to win numerous awards around the country. Above is the cast of *'Johnny Belinda'*, the winning entry at the Felixstowe Drama Festival in 1950.

132. A further picture of Tredegar Amateur Dramatic Society showing members and committee with some trophies in 1950.

133. The First World War ended with the armistice on November 11th 1918, a conflict that cost the lives of some 300 men from the Tredegar District. It was some years later before the inclination and funds became available to erect a suitable monument. The picture on the left shows Lord Tredegar at the unveiling of the town's War Memorial in Bedwellty Park on December 14th 1924.

134. There may well be some former members of the Merrymakers pictured here in 1941 who can recognise some faces on this war-time photograph.

135. The last passenger train ran from Abergavenny to Merthyr on January 5th 1958, ending almost a hundred years of railway history. The Stephenson Locomotive Society Special is seen here on its last call at Nantybwch. Nearest the engine is Mr. Harse senior, accompanied by Mr. Ewart Harse and his young child.

136. Dismantling of the rail track in front of Glyn Terrace Tredegar. Among the workers are Jack Milton, Fred Whitcombe and Ron Abbot. This rail track took the waste slag from the T.I.C. Works to the tip at Brompton.

137./138. Two local carnival events are recalled in these pictures. Firstly, a group of ladies from Georgetown are marching up Stable Lane and the second photograph was taken at Scwrfa Carnival in the 1950s.

139. The committee of the British Legion Club provides a few faces to be remembered from the year 1958. Left to right are, back row: Jack Neal, Jocky Wise, Eddy Loader, Bill Thompson, Watty Powell, Teddy Marsh, Warren Jenkins and Ken Lloyd. Front row: Dai Collins, Duker Jones, Peter Padfield, Maisie and Eddie Hamer, Jim Beeks and Bill Powell.

140. A pilgrimage to the 'International' at Dublin in 1956 with the Tredegar supporters about to board the first Viscount Aircraft to depart from Rhoose Airport. Among the pilgrims are Ken Brown, Bill Morris, Alec Jackson, Cliff Sullivan, Jim Driscoll, Bryn Bevan, Bert Bethel, Joe Beynon, Fred Jenkins, Bill Dean, Basil Eynon, Colin Lewis, Sam Oliver, Tom Lewis, Gilbert Needs, Joe Moon, Ivor and Tom Constable, John Price, Babe Evans, Ron Lewis, Don Jones, Vernon Shore, Mel Hughes, Bill McGrath, Terry Callaghan and Arthur Vaughan.

145. Dukestown Home Guard pictured during the 1939-45 War, based at St. George's Parish Hall, Dukestown Road. This photograph was taken in the yard of the Sirhowy Ironworks. Some faces have been identified and these are Doug Robinson, Tom Short, Reg Jones, Ken Shepherd, Bill Edwards, Reg Simmonds, Stan Jones and Vernon Shaw.

146. Many young members seen here belong to the Tabernacle Concert Party at Dukestown. This was another collection of strong local talent who once entertained in the district and beyond.

139. The committee of the British Legion Club provides a few faces to be remembered from the year 1958. Left to right are, back row: Jack Neal, Jocky Wise, Eddy Loader, Bill Thompson, Watty Powell, Teddy Marsh, Warren Jenkins and Ken Lloyd. Front row: Dai Collins, Duker Jones, Peter Padfield, Maisie and Eddie Hamer, Jim Beeks and Bill Powell.

140. A pilgrimage to the 'International' at Dublin in 1956 with the Tredegar supporters about to board the first Viscount Aircraft to depart from Rhoose Airport. Among the pilgrims are Ken Brown, Bill Morris, Alec Jackson, Cliff Sullivan, Jim Driscoll, Bryn Bevan, Bert Bethel, Joe Beynon, Fred Jenkins, Bill Dean, Basil Eynon, Colin Lewis, Sam Oliver, Tom Lewis, Gilbert Needs, Joe Moon, Ivor and Tom Constable, John Price, Babe Evans, Ron Lewis, Don Jones, Vernon Shore, Mel Hughes, Bill McGrath, Terry Callaghan and Arthur Vaughan.

145. Dukestown Home Guard pictured during the 1939-45 War, based at St. George's Parish Hall, Dukestown Road. This photograph was taken in the yard of the Sirhowy Ironworks. Some faces have been identified and these are Doug Robinson, Tom Short, Reg Jones, Ken Shepherd, Bill Edwards, Reg Simmonds, Stan Jones and Vernon Shaw.

146. Many young members seen here belong to the Tabernacle Concert Party at Dukestown. This was another collection of strong local talent who once entertained in the district and beyond.

139. The committee of the British Legion Club provides a few faces to be remembered from the year 1958. Left to right are, back row: Jack Neal, Jocky Wise, Eddy Loader, Bill Thompson, Watty Powell, Teddy Marsh, Warren Jenkins and Ken Lloyd. Front row: Dai Collins, Duker Jones, Peter Padfield, Maisie and Eddie Hamer, Jim Beeks and Bill Powell.

140. A pilgrimage to the 'International' at Dublin in 1956 with the Tredegar supporters about to board the first Viscount Aircraft to depart from Rhoose Airport. Among the pilgrims are Ken Brown, Bill Morris, Alec Jackson, Cliff Sullivan, Jim Driscoll, Bryn Bevan, Bert Bethel, Joe Beynon, Fred Jenkins, Bill Dean, Basil Eynon, Colin Lewis, Sam Oliver, Tom Lewis, Gilbert Needs, Joe Moon, Ivor and Tom Constable, John Price, Babe Evans, Ron Lewis, Don Jones, Vernon Shore, Mel Hughes, Bill McGrath, Terry Callaghan and Arthur Vaughan.

141. The Tredegar Operatic Society pictured in the Lesser Hall at the Workmen's Institute. Dormant for many years, the choral society was resurrected by popular demand and given new financial support by the Workmen's Institute Society in 1947. The picture above is from about the mid 1960s.

142. A ladies' rugby team and one or two male supporters from Rhoslan, Sirhowy at an event in 1969.

143. Proud and in full regalia are these officers of the Tredegar Branch of the Royal Order of the Buffs during the 1920s. Front row, left to right: Billy Earle (Manager of Hipps Clothing Store), Bill Jennings, George Mowberry (Master Baker of Temple Street), Mr Powell (Manager of Harris Temple of Fashion, Commercial Street). Unfortunately none of the back row have been identified.

144. In 1851 a plan was conceived to extract the largest lump of coal possible, from a local level as Tredegar's contribution to the Great Exhibition at Crystal Palace. After great toil by the colliers a lump weighing 20 tons was recovered, only to break whilst being loaded onto a wagon. To the dismay of many, the idea was abandoned and the remaining piece weighing about 10 tons was preserved at Bedwellty Park. This photograph shows a similar exercise in 1951 when a lump weighing 2 tons was taken from a Sirhowy level; this was for the Festival of Britain held in London that year.

145. Dukestown Home Guard pictured during the 1939-45 War, based at St. George's Parish Hall, Dukestown Road. This photograph was taken in the yard of the Sirhowy Ironworks. Some faces have been identified and these are Doug Robinson, Tom Short, Reg Jones, Ken Shepherd, Bill Edwards, Reg Simmonds, Stan Jones and Vernon Shaw.

146. Many young members seen here belong to the Tabernacle Concert Party at Dukestown. This was another collection of strong local talent who once entertained in the district and beyond.

CHAPTER 5

Shops & Traders

147. Commercial Street began to develop as an area for traders to sell their wares in the mid 1870s. Until that period it was marked on the map as Colliers Row. This picture from around 1904, shows quite a large Pegler's grocery shop, with Broomhalls next door purveying 'tea and presents'.

148. The latter-day boot and shoe shop of Mr. Price and Son in Commercial Street. On display are samples of shoe leather which customers could select and have their boots made on the premises.

149. Up until the early 1960s ice cream was available from the horse-drawn cart of Mr. Zeraschi. The little girl is seen here at Rhyd Terrace.

150. The once-popular horse and trap, private transport for those who could afford the luxury. Sat on the trap is Mr. Rake who had an auctioneering business in Church Street. The public house is thought to be the Top House at Trevil.

151. A scene outside Dukestown Provision Stores, a one-time busy shop which stood in Picton Road. Standing in front of the delivery cart is Mr. Johnathan Philips, the shop-owner.

152. Another old and established business that once stood in Castle Street was Swabricks. It's not certain who the ladies are stood at the door but the shop was a popular printers and stationers.

153. With the amount of heavy industry in Tredegar there would have been quite a demand for sturdy footwear in the early days. Here is a picture of Price's boot and shop with the staff outside. The premises were situated by the yard gates at the top of Church Street and known as Bristol House.

154. At the beginning of the twentieth century, if one could afford it, the final journey could be made in great style. Above is seen a picture that was used to promote the services and luxurious horse-drawn hearse of Messrs. 'Vaughan Brothers, Tredegar Funeral Director'.

155. The defunct railway station at Tredegar, pictured here in 1964 when it was used by Messrs. D.H. Davies as storage space for Vauxhall cars and vans. In the background can be seen the old T.I.C. offices. The old station and railway lines now form the route of the town's by-pass.

160. Only the more mature readers are likely to remember this gentleman. His name was Harry Oliver and he was a popular tradesman of the town, delivering coal direct to the customers' doors by horse and cart for well over twenty years until the 1950s. Probably the majority of homes in Tredegar are now heated by gas, much easier than handling the lumps of coal seen on Harry's cart!

161. Aneurin Morgan and Son with a display of bicycles outside their shop in Commercial Street. Next door was once the town's Chinese Laundry with Thomas the Chemist on the other side. Occupying these premises now are Proberts Greengrocers and Daisy Chain the Florist.

FROM THE
PHOTOGRAPHIC
Studio
OF
W. Clayton.
Art
Photographer
Iron Street.
Tredegar.

COPIES CAN BE HAD.

162. Not easily identifiable but this was once a little shop situated at the bottom of Charles Street. The photograph probably dates from the 1930s so perhaps the young children are alive and well and maybe, even reading this book.

163. The electrical and radio shop of J.C. Charles in Castle Street. This establishment also served as motor engineers in early times as evidenced by a fuel pump, rather unusually in the doorway! The company having traded in the town for many years now have premises in Commercial Street.

164. Jervis's shop once at the bottom of Sirhowy Hill. Seen here in 1930 are George Rake, Ray Jervis, Charlie Wilbrum and James Jervis.

165. Outside the Full Moon, Scwrfa with landlord James Jervis accompanied by Doris Moore, Maud, Marie and Ray Jervis.

166. The ancient Fountain Inn or 'The Farm' as it is known these days. The gentleman seen here is Mr. Alfred Thomas who was landlord at the time.

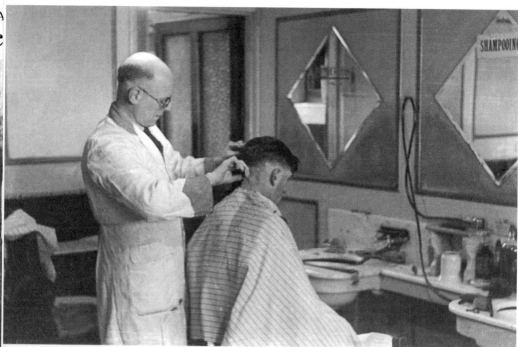

167. Local residents will know of 'Dai the Barber' who is seen here creating a hairstyle commonly referred to as a 'short back and sides'. This barber's shop was situated where the new post office now stands in Commercial Street.

168. The Progressive Club and Institute which once stood next to the yard gates at the top of Church Street. In later years it became Toppings Wool Shop and a furniture store for Jack Derrick. The site is now completely cleared.

177. From probably more than forty years ago is this school photograph taken in the gymnasium at the Grammar School. The teacher on this occasion is Mr. Scandrett.

178. The football team of Sirhowy School proudly display a trophy won during the 1951-52 season. The teacher on the left is Mr. Meyrick and on the right is Mr. Wilcox.

187./188. The original photograph would have been taken in 1954-55 so the pupils today would age from about 54 to 60. Former pupils will now wish to ponder and identify themselves, school chums and respected teachers.

189. The final photograph of the quintet and if any reader has attempted the count of faces, there are 179 girls, 168 boys and 19 members of staff.

190. The Thomas Richards Technical School in 1948 and where possible the boys have been named. Front row, left to right:- Dennis Marks, Graham Hurley, Ken Owen, John Neads, Brian Smith, unknown, Graham Hall, unknown and Howard Price. Second row: Michael Cadwallader, Donald Morgan, Victor Greenwood, Tony Coles, Brian Prescott, unknown, Raymond George, William Bass and David Nevins. Third row: John McQuade, Thornton Jones, Gerald Whitehorn, Colin Griffiths, Gordon Snelgrove, Selwyn Morgan, John Harper, Melville Evans and unknown. Back row: Hilling Davies, Trevor Dowdsewell, Alan George, Gwyn Llewellyn, Keith Lloyd, David Thomas, Douglas Roberts and Tecwyn George.

191. Boys and girls of Sirhowy Mixed School in 1930. The school was originally opened in about 1840 by the Sirhowy Company, being influenced by the success of the Tredegar Iron Company's school in the Town Hall. The Education Act of 1870 which introduced compulsory elementary education for all, was eventually to put an end to the control that the ironmasters had over the seats of learning.

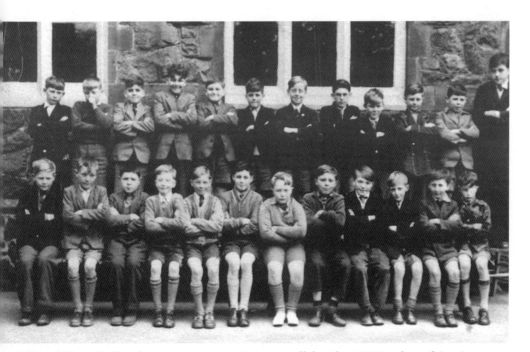

192. Although the date is uncertain, it may well be the 1950s when this picture was taken at Georgetown School. This School was opened in 1876 under the authority of the newly formed School Board, which superseded the private teaching establishments in the area.

193. Another photograph from Georgetown School, this time the soccer team of 1948-49. On the right is the familiar face of teacher Mr. Padfield.

194. The Drama Group at the Grammar School during the 1950s.

Sport & Recreation

195./196. Another scene from the bygone days of Tredegar, the very popular open air swimming pool. During the depression years of the 1930s, a number of schemes were put into operation to try and ease the critical unemployment situation. With Government approval, Tredegar Council authorised the building of a magnificent swimming pool which opened to the public in 1932. By today's standards of course it would be very   antiquated but, during its first season alone, the project attracted 115,000 swimmers and spectators. Closed some years ago there is little evidence left to show that it ever existed in the park.

197. The Tredegar Air Training Corps Football Team 1945-1946. Seen left to right are, back row: Dick Bridgeman (Trainer), Spencer Lane, Vic Longden, Alan Williams, Sam Oliver, Murray Jackson, Len Phillips, Don Jones and Mr. Llew Harry. Middle row: Ron Lane, Ian Sheen, Bill Penny, Eddie Pugh, Ken Sheen (Captain), Alan Sullivan, Vernon Jenkins and Ray Bridgeman. Front row: Dennis Turner and Ritchie Evans.

198. A cricket team from the Grammar School photographed during the 1950s.

199. Two photographs of the sportsmen of Glanhowy. Above is seen a football team from the Youth Club in the 1950s, with youth leader Mr. Harry Harris on the far right.

200. Glanhowy Youth Rugby Team 1964-65. Back row, left to right: Roger Thomas, Dai Griffiths, John Thomas, Neil Evans, Gary Palfrey, Ron Williams, John Cullen, Neil Durham, Ian Morgan, Harry Harris and Ron Davies. Middle row: Gerald Freeman, Bernard Stevens, Colin James (Captain), Roy 'Spud' Jones and Gerald Cartwright. Front row: Alwyn Robertson and Trevor Denham.

201. Outside the Crown Public House is the venue for the Ashvale Football Club. The year is 1952, obviously a successful season judging by the array of cups and trophies on display.

202. A troop of St. George's Cub Scouts outside the scout headquarters on Farmers Hill, Scwfra in 1939. Some readers may recognise the houses in the background which belong to Howells Terrace, Dukestown.

203. A pre-nourishment photograph at the annual dinner at the Conservative Club Cricket Team in 1954.

204. Some more familiar faces when the Globe Inn Darts Team gather for the winners' presentation dinner in 1952. The Globe is another of the town's public houses to have vanished. It used to stand in Church Street where the flats are these days.

205./206. Some pictures from some dedicated followers of rugby in the district. Above is Tredegar R.F.C. in the early 1970s whilst below are members of the Compton Electric Car Company team in 1972.

207. Tredegar Ironsides and officials who can be named are as follows - Back row, left to right: G. Evans, T. Gregory, G. Shaw, J. Wilkes, R. Miles and W. Weaver. Middle row: W. Gregory, R. Clay, B. Thomas, D. Hunt, T. Gregory, C. Sheehy, J. Titley, D. Owen, D. Harris, P. Weeks and J. Gregory (Chairman). Front row: J. Zeraschi, W. Jenkins, R. Evans, P. Wilkes, K. Griffiths, J. Price, K. Marsh, R. Giles and J. Evans. In foreground: L. Durham and C. Rixon.

208. Some more cups on display on behalf of Scwrfa A.F.C. in 1949-50.

209. The Youth Club members of Glanhowy whilst on a visit to Germany during the 1950s.

210. 1971 and it's presentation night for sportsmen of a different kind. This time it is the turn of the Sirhowy Angling Club to receive their presentations. Some of the names on the photograph are Vince Miles, Terry Palfrey, Ritchie Palfrey, Roy Rees, Jeff Perrin, Keith Price and Ray James.

118

211. Trefil Rugby Football Club winners of the Cyrus Davies Cup in the 1964-65 season. Seeen here are, back row, left to right: G. Duggan, T. Davies, C. Bevan, V. Millar, B. Davies, M. Dwyer, R. Davies, R. Weeks, W. Harris, T. Jones and G. Williams. Centre row: D. Davies (Vice Captain), G. James, R. Davies (Captain), T. Jewel and B. Shankland. Front row: G. Thomas, F. Davies, C. Davies and G. Hodnett.

212. Even the local bus company could muster a football team at one time. This soccer 'eleven' are employees of the Red and White Bus Company in the 1950s.

213. Now it is the ladies' turn to pose for the photographer. These hockey players are from the Grammar School in the 1950s.

214. An annual dinner for Tredegar RFC in the early 1970s and joining some of the players are, front row, left to right: Wally Talbot (Chairman, Mon R.F.C.), Charlie Butler (Captain), Sam Beynon (Chairman), Mel Bevan (Player of the Year), Cllr. B. White (Chairman of UDC) and David Jones (Clubman of Year).

CHAPTER 8

Scenes Past & Present

215./216. This final chapter contains a small number of photographs to assist some younger readers in understanding the extensive changes that have affected various parts of Tredegar over the years.

Some 70 years separate these two photographs taken at the top of Morgan Street, the old Olympia Cinema these days being used as commercial premises.

217./218. Commercial Street pictured from the same spot at the turn of the century and again in 1998 having been pedestrianised. The large building on the right of the upper photograph was Tredegar's Co-op Store which was demolished a few years ago. The new road system leading into the modern car park and shopping precinct now occupy this area.

219./220. Only more mature readers can remember that the town ever possessed a railway station and the lower picture shows its former whereabouts. The whole site is now replaced by the by-pass and roundabout.

221./222.   This picturesque and rural scene looking towards Robbins Farm and The Nine Arches will bring back some wonderful memories for some readers. This area provided a popular walk through the meadow to go picnicking at the Weir and Nine Arches. The scene today has been transformed into the private housing estate of Dukes Meadow.

223./224. Easily recognisable above is the Workmen's Hall and Cinema which had stood in the town from 1861 until demolition in 1995. All evidence has been removed and the visual remains consist of yet another car park.

225./226. The above scene is one that the younger generation will fail to recognise, that part of town which was known as The Yard Gates. There was an important level crossing and gates here, to allow trucks loaded with limestone from Trefil quarry to make their way to the Tredegar Ironworks. The scene below is what we have in 1998.

227./228. What a difference a road makes to the rural countryside as illustrated in these two photographs which were taken from exactly the same spot, just below The Nine Arches. Above, the period is the early 1960s, the Heads of The Valley Road is at the planning stage and the result is seen below. Within the next year or two the picture is set to change once more as the road widening scheme comes into operation.

Acknowledgements

Acknowledgements are due to the undermentioned who kindly loaned some of their own photographs and information for inclusion in this book. Sincere apologies are extended to anyone who may have been inadvertently omitted.

Terry Baines, David Beeks, Mel Bevan, John Briggs, Tom Brown, W.A.Camwell, Tony Clay, Ralph Cousins, Alwyn Davies, Barrie Davies, Gerald Davies, Rae Davies, Howard Dwyer, David Edwards, Brenda Gould, Philip Griffiths, Granville Hall, Derrick Harding, Ewart Harse, Philip Havard, Gordon Hayward, Colin James, Ray Jervis, Trevor Jones (The Milk), Roland N. Lewis, Sylvia Lewis, Roly Morgan, Sam Oliver, Bernard (Barny) Phillips, Leighton Pritchard, Harold Rattigan, Brian Roberts, W.W. Tasker, Malcolm Thomas, Tredegar Ironsides R.F.C., Trefil R.F.C., Mary Walby, June Zeraschi.

Below is a selection of further titles available. Please send stamp to the Publishers for a detailed catalogue.

Blackwood Yesterday in Photographs — **Book 1**
by Ewart Smith ISBN 0 9512181 6 6
Blackwood Yesterday in Photographs — **Book 2**
by Ewart Smith ISBN 1 874538 65 4
Blackwood Yesterday in Photographs — **Book 3**
by Ewart Smith ISBN 1 874538 76 X
A Portrait of Rhymney — **Volume 1**
by Marion Evans ISBN 0 874538 40 9
A Portrait of Rhymney — **Volume 2**
by Marion Evans ISBN 1 874538 70 0
A Portrait of Rhymney — **Volume 3**
by Marion Evans ISBN 1 874538 41 7
Brynmawr, Beaufort and Blaina in Photographs — **Volume 1**
by Malcolm Thomas ISBN 1 874538 15 8
Brynmawr, Beaufort and Blaina in Photographs — **Volume 2**
by Malcolm Thomas ISBN 1 874538 26 3
Trinant in Photographs — **Volume 1**
by Clive Daniels ISBN 1 874538 80 8
Collieries of the Sirhowy Valley
by Rayner Rosser ISBN 1 874538 01 8
The Flavour of Islwyn Remembered
by Kay Jenkins ISBN 1 874538 06 9
Bargoed & Gilfach in Photographs — **Volume 1**
by Paul James ISBN 1 874538 31 X
History of Webbs Brewery - Aberbeeg
by Ray Morris ISBN 1 874538 46 8
A Look at Old Tredegar in Photographs — **Volume 1**
by Philip Prosser ISBN 0 9512181 4 X
A History of Fochriw in Photographs — **Volume 1**
by Peter Price ISBN 1 874538 11 5
A History of Fochriw in Photographs — **Volume 2**
by Peter Price ISBN 1 874538 56 5
Hills of Fire and Iron
by Peter Morgan Jones ISBN 0 9512181 9 0
Remember Abergavenny — **Volume 1**
by Louis Bannon ISBN 1 874538 75 1
Caerleon 'Scenes Past' — **Volume 1**
by Norman Stevens ISBN 1 874538 71 9
A Picture Book of Cwm — **Volume 1**
by Margaret Blackwell ISBN 1 874538 66 2
The Places Names of Eastern Gwent
by Graham Osborne & Graham Hobbs ISBN 1 874538 91 3